Little Red Riding Hood

Le Petit Chaperon Rouge

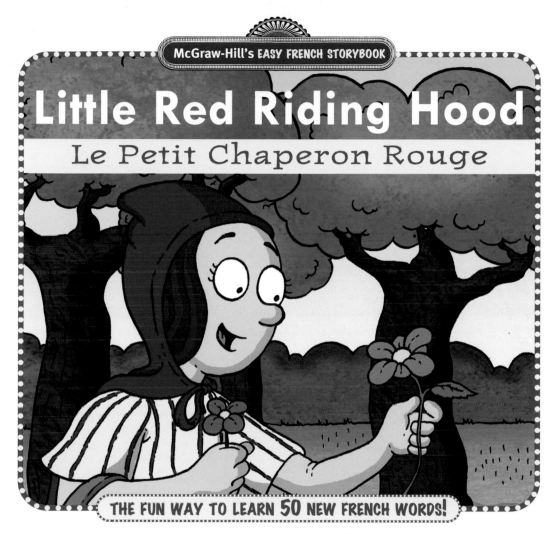

THE FUN WAY TO LEARN 50 NEW FRENCH WORDS!

Ana Lomba

Illustrated by Santiago Cornejo • French Translation by Dominique Wenzel • Audio Produced by Rob Zollman

McGraw-Hill

New York   Chicago   San Francisco   Lisbon   London   Madrid   Mexico City
Milan   New Delhi   San Juan   Seoul   Singapore   Sydney   Toronto

1 2 3 4 5 6 7 8 9 0   CTP/CTP   0 9 8 7 6 5

ISBN 0-07-146167-1 (book and CD)
ISBN 0-07-146168-X (book alone)
Library of Congress Control Number: 2005927570

Interior design by General Learning Communications

McGraw-Hill books are available at special quantity discounts to use as premiums and sales promotions, or for use in corporate training programs. For more information, please write to the Director of Special Sales, Professional Publishing, McGraw-Hill, Two Penn Plaza, New York, NY 10121-2298. Or contact your local bookstore.

A mon mari, John Mulcahy,

parce que tu crois en mes rêves et que tu t'y associes.

Affectueusement.

To my husband, John Mulcahy,

because you believe in my dreams and join in them.

With love.

Introduction

Welcome to the world of **easy and fun** French for young children!

Young children learn languages best when they are active participants—just as they learned their native language. Children learning a second language in a classroom or structured setting do not have the same opportunities to hear and use the language as they have for their native language. Parents can offer important supplemental exposure by providing high-quality language instruction at home. The target language introduced needs to be age appropriate and engaging so children can use it (and will want to use it) in different situations.

McGraw-Hill's Easy French Storybooks are designed to smoothly immerse children in French by using simple narration and everyday dialogues to relate familiar stories, accompanied by illustrations that help tell the story. By creating a direct link between the story lines and the illustrations, children can infer meaning from both text and images, leading to greater understanding. Moreover, the use of common, everyday language exchanges in the stories eases children's language acquisition. *McGraw-Hill's Easy French Storybooks* contain the proper amount of conversational language for a beginning level of instruction.

Start by referring to the mini-picture dictionary at the end of the book. Point to the illustrations as you listen to the vocabulary words on the companion CD. After listening a few times, test the children's comprehension by asking them to point to the illustrations as you say the words. Change the order of the words to ensure comprehension.

Ask simple questions like *Qui est-ce?* (Who is it?) or *Qu'est-ce que c'est?* (What is it?) to elicit verbal responses. If your children don't respond, offer the answer. Children need time to figure out the links between the new words and concepts, as well as to register and practice new sounds. So encourage, but don't force speaking. Praise goes a long way; make sure to use lots of compliments: *Très bien!* (Very good!)

It is not necessary to know all the vocabulary in the mini-picture dictionary to start listening to the story. You can first listen to the English version of the story if that will help you become familiar with the story. Once you start reading the French story, I recommend sticking to French. Do not switch back and forth between languages. If you do this, your children may not make the effort to understand and learn French.

Listen to the French story several times. After you're familiar with it, start reading the story in French to your children. Don't let pronunciation stop you. You will become more proficient with practice. Your children will have a big advantage over you in pronunciation, as they are able to hear and register sounds that you cannot distinguish—consider this a "blind spot" in your hearing because you were not exposed to those sounds earlier in life. Use a lot of expression and animation. Your children will love to see you speaking French! If your children can read on their own, you may want to let them read the book themselves.

The story in this book is very theatrical. In my classes, teachers become actors: they impersonate the protagonists of the story and transform the classroom into a stage. In one-on-one situations you can jazz up the story by using puppets or acting out the story yourself. I have observed in my classes that children become more talkative when they are using puppets or masks. This gives them more freedom, as they can act as somebody else! The use of puppets or masks is an excellent strategy for shy children. Create a make-believe corner in your home with puppets, masks, and costumes related to the story. This allows children to explore the new language hands-on in spontaneous play.

To further expand learning, use *McGraw-Hill's Easy French Storybooks* in combination with *Play and Learn French* (available from McGraw-Hill). *Play and Learn French*, also based on our "easy immersion" methodology, contains conversations, games, and songs that you can use with your children every day. You can also enjoy *McGraw-Hill's Easy French Storybook: Goldilocks and the Three Bears / Boucle d'Or et les trois ours.*

Enjoy discovering new worlds together!

Le Petit Chaperon Rouge vivait avec sa maman dans une petite maison très jolie.

Little Red Riding Hood lived with her mom in a very beautiful little house.

Un jour sa maman lui dit, *"Petit Chaperon Rouge,
ta grand-mère est malade."*

One day her mom said to Little Red Riding Hood,
"Little Red Riding Hood, Grandma is sick."

"S'il te plaît, porte-lui ce panier."
"Très bien, maman," dit le Petit Chaperon Rouge.

"Please, take this basket to her."
"OK, Mom," said Little Red Riding Hood.

3

Le Petit Chaperon Rouge marchait dans la forêt quand, soudain, un méchant loup sortit de derrière un arbre.

Little Red Riding Hood was walking in the forest when, all of a sudden, a bad wolf came out from behind a tree.

"Petit Chaperon Rouge, où vas-tu?"
dit le loup.
"Je vais chez ma grand-mère,"
répondit le Petit Chaperon Rouge.

"Little Red Riding Hood, where are you going?" said the wolf.
"I am going to my grandma's house," answered Little Red
Riding Hood.

"Et où habite ta grand-mère?"
"Là-bas."

"And where does your grandma live?"
"Over there."

"Au revoir, Petit Chaperon Rouge. À bientôt."
"Au revoir, Monsieur le Loup."

"Good-bye, Little Red Riding Hood. See you soon."
"Good-bye, Mr. Wolf."

Le Petit Chaperon Rouge marchait
lentement, très lentement...
"Une fleur jaune. Qu'elle est jolie!"

Little Red Riding Hood was walking slowly, very slowly . . .
"A yellow flower. How beautiful!"

... et le loup courait et courait.

. . . and the wolf ran and ran.

Le Petit Chaperon Rouge marchait lentement,
très lentement...
"Une fleur rouge. Qu'elle est jolie!"

Little Red Riding Hood was walking slowly, very slowly . . .
"A red flower. How beautiful!"

... et le loup courait et courait.

. . . . and the wolf ran and ran.

Le Petit Chaperon Rouge marchait lentement,
très lentement...
"Une fleur violette. Qu'elle est jolie!"

Little Red Riding Hood was walking slowly, very slowly . . .
"A purple flower. How beautiful!"

... et le loup courait et courait.

. . . and the wolf ran and ran.

Le loup arriva très fatigué à la maison
de la grand-mère.
"Ah, ah, ah."
Toc, toc.

The wolf arrived very tired at Grandma's house.
"Ah, ah, ah."
Knock, knock.

"*Qui est là?*" dit la grand-mère.
"*C'est moi, le Petit Chaperon Rouge,*" répondit le loup.
"*Entre, entre, mon enfant.*"

"Who is it?" said Grandma.
"It's me, Little Red Riding Hood," answered the wolf.
"Come in, come in, dear."

**Le loup entra, claqua la porte (*Vlan!*)
et mangea la grand-mère.**

The wolf came in, slammed the door (*Bang!*),
and ate up Grandma.

"**Pouah, elle n'était pas bonne du tout, la grand-mère! Et j'ai encore faim... Petit Chaperon Rouge!**" dit le loup en se léchant les babines.

"Yikes, I didn't like Grandma at all! And I'm still hungry . . . Little Red Riding Hood!" said the wolf, licking his lips.

Le loup enfila une chemise de nuit, un bonnet et des lunettes et se mit dans le lit. *"Que je suis beau!"*

The wolf put on a nightgown, a hat, and glasses, and got into bed. "I look so handsome!"

18

Pendant ce temps, le Petit Chaperon Rouge marchait lentement, très lentement, à travers la forêt. *"Une fleur énorme. Qu'elle est jolie!"*

Meanwhile, Little Red Riding Hood was walking slowly, very slowly, through the forest.
"A huge flower. How beautiful!"

Le Petit Chaperon Rouge arriva — enfin! — chez sa grand-mère. Toc, toc.

Little Red Riding Hood arrived — finally! — at Grandma's house. Knock, knock.

"Qui est là?" dit le loup.
"C'est moi, le Petit Chaperon Rouge," répondit le Petit Chaperon Rouge.
"Entre, entre, mon enfant."

"Who is it?" said the wolf.
"It's me, Little Red Riding Hood," answered Little Red Riding Hood.
"Come in, come in, dear."

"Grand-mère, grand-mère, que tu as de grands yeux!" dit le Petit Chaperon Rouge. **"C'est pour mieux te voir, mon enfant,"** dit le loup.

"Grandma, Grandma, what big eyes you have!" said Little Red Riding Hood.
"The better to see you with, my dear," said the wolf.

"Grand-mère, grand-mère, que tu as un grand nez!"
"C'est pour mieux te sentir, mon enfant."

"Grandma, Grandma, what a big nose you have!"
"The better to smell you with, my dear."

**"Grand-mère, grand-mère,
que tu as de grandes oreilles!"
"C'est pour mieux t'entendre, mon enfant."**

"Grandma, Grandma, what big ears you have!"
"The better to hear you with, my dear."

"Grand-mère, grand-mère, que tu as de grandes dents!"
"C'est pour mieux te manger!"

"Grandma, Grandma, what big teeth you have!"
"The better to eat you with!"

Le loup mangea le Petit Chaperon Rouge en une
seule bouchée.
*"Le Petit Chaperon Rouge était délicieuse,
mais j'ai encore faim... Un panier!"*

The wolf ate up Little Red Riding Hood in a single bite.
"Little Red Riding Hood was very tasty, but I am still hungry . . .
A basket!"

"*Voyons... du poulet! J'aime bien le poulet. C'est délicieux!*"

"Let's see . . . chicken! I like chicken. How yummy!"

"Voyons... du lait! Je n'aime pas le lait. C'est dégoûtant! Allez, ouste!"

"Let's see . . . milk! I don't like milk. How disgusting! Get out!"

"**Voyons... du beurre! Je n'aime pas
le beurre. C'est dégoûtant! Allez, ouste.**"

"Let's see . . . butter! I don't like butter. How disgusting! Get out!"

"*Voyons... du pain! J'aime bien le pain.
C'est délicieux!*"

"Let's see . . . bread! I like bread. How yummy!"

Après avoir tant mangé le loup eut très sommeil.
"Que j'ai sommeil! Et que j'ai le ventre plein!"
dit-il, et il s'endormit.

After eating so much the wolf felt very sleepy. "I am so sleepy!
And I am so full!" he said, and he fell asleep.

Peu de temps après, un bûcheron passa par là et entendit les ronflements du loup.

"Que c'est bizarre!" dit-il. "Je vais entrer voir si la grand-mère va bien."

Later, a woodcutter passed by and heard the snores of the wolf. "How strange!" he said. "I'll go in and check if Grandma is all right."

Le bûcheron vit le loup endormi et entendit des cris qui venaient de son ventre.
"A l'aide! Au secours!"

The woodcutter saw the sleeping wolf and heard screams coming from his belly.
"Help! Help!"

Le bûcheron prit sa hache et (*Pan!*) il ouvrit le ventre du loup. Le Petit Chaperon Rouge et sa grand-mère sortirent couvertes de nourriture. ***"C'est dégoûtant!"***

The woodcutter got his ax and (*Whack!*) he cut open the wolf's belly. Little Red Riding Hood and Grandma came out covered in food. "How disgusting!"

Le bûcheron, le Petit Chaperon Rouge et la grand-mère remplirent de pierres le ventre du loup…
"Donne-moi encore des pierres."

The woodcutter, Little Red Riding Hood, and Grandma filled up the wolf's belly with stones . . .
"Give me more stones."

... et ils se cachèrent derrière un arbre pour voir ce qui se passait.

. . . and hid behind a tree to see what happened.

Le loup se réveilla. *"Que je me sens lourd!*
J'ai trop mangé!"

The wolf woke up. "I feel so heavy! I ate too much!"

Le loup se mit à marcher lentement, très lentement, et il ne revint plus jamais dans la forêt. *"Aïe, que je suis malade!"*

The wolf walked away slowly, very slowly, and he never came back to the forest. "Ugh, I'm so sick!"

Le bûcheron, le Petit Chaperon Rouge et la grand-mère s'assirent pour manger du poulet, du lait, des carottes, du pain et du beurre.
"C'est délicieux!" dirent-ils tous.
Voilà, c'est la fin de l'histoire.

The woodcutter, Little Red Riding Hood, and Grandma
sat down to eat chicken, milk, carrots, bread, and butter.
"How yummy!" they all said.
The End.

la fille (le Petit Chaperon Rouge)

girl (Little Red Riding Hood)

la grand-mère

grandmother

le loup

wolf

la chemise de nuit

nightgown

le bonnet

hat

les lunettes

glasses

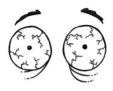

les yeux

eyes

les oreilles

ears

les dents

teeth

le poulet

chicken

le beurre

butter

le bûcheron

woodcutter

About the Author

Award-winning, language-learning innovator Ana Lomba is the founder and director of Sueños de Colores LLC, a company offering language-learning instruction and resources for parents and teachers of young children. She is the coauthor of the books *Play and Learn Spanish* and *Play and Learn French*, published by McGraw-Hill, 2005 Parents' Choice Approved award winners. Ana is an advocate for early foreign language education and holds leadership positions in prominent U.S. regional and national language associations, including the American Council on the Teaching of Foreign Languages (ACTFL), the National Network for Early Language Learning (NNELL), and Foreign Language Educators of New Jersey (FLENJ). Ana holds advanced degrees in Spanish and Latin American literature from Binghamton University and Princeton University. A native of Madrid, Spain, Ana currently lives with her husband and three children in Princeton, New Jersey.